THE A
JOURNEY

From Darkness to Light

To Sally,
Keep making a difference in
our World.
Blessing

Elliott J. Kelly

WRITTEN BY:
ELLIOTT G. KELLY

THE AWAITED JOURNEY

From Darkness to Light

Published by

EGK Publishing, Houston, Texas

© Copyright 2011 by Elliott G. Kelly

WRITTEN BY:
ELLIOTT G. KELLY

THE AWAITED JOURNEY

DEDICATION

I owe a great debt to my parents, Bennie and Alma Kelly, for their unconditional love and understanding. Their patience made a great difference in my life as I began to turn away from what they had originally envisioned for me.

To my father, thank you for being "The Rock" of our family. Even though you are a man of few words, your quiet yet stern presence has blessed our family tremendously. Like Jeremiah the Prophet, when you spoke, your family listened.

To my mother, you are one of the most loving and patient women that I know. I want to thank you for being my editor (the first) during all my studies and for encouraging me to finish what I started.

To my big brother, Myron, thank you for always being my protector.

ACKNOWLEDGEMENTS

Lois Martin, Thank you for embracing my story and igniting my inspiration to write.

Kathi Mancini, words can't even express my gratitude for your enthusiasm to take my life story and transform it into this work of art. You have been so exceptional to work with and I can't wait for our next project together.

Jerome Dura'n, Wow! What an amazing job you have done! You have taken my ideas and turned them into this wonderful masterpiece.

Valerie Peterson, Thank you for coaching me to the finish line and being a fresh pair of eyes to the pages that I have written.

INVENTORY

OF MY LIFE

Forward

CROSSROAD

Do I really have access to you, "God"? You said that I can come to you at anytime. Can you hear me, Lord? Can you hear my cry? I am in deep pain. This pain that I have is getting deeper. Reach down and pull me up, Lord. I can't see. It is too dark. My sinful ways are hidden deep in my soul. You said you will not remember them. I know you love me, Lord, because you bless me with shoes to go from here to there.

Do you love me that much; that you would do that for me? But, I am so different! People will make fun of my voice. They say I don't sound like the others. Can you use me like Moses? He had a stick and a stutter. Will they follow me? I will go where you tell me. I'm tired, Lord. I have been made fun of, beat up, tossed up and scorned.

Bathe me, Lord! Wash me clean! I don't like the smell down here. I am lost, not knowing where to go or where to turn. I listen to my friends, but pay you no mind. Can you get me out of this place? What do you want me to do, Lord? I promise I will listen this time.

This is my story of crossing life's intersections in rush hour traffic. Although there were many twists and turns in the road; all led to the discovery of my place, where the Kingdom of Heaven collides with the mindset of mankind here on Earth.

ONE

THE NAMELESS AND FACELESS HEROES OF MY TIME

As a child, I was influenced by teachers from school, members of my church, and even people in my neighborhood, none of which are famous, and some whose names escape me. But their views and opinions effected how I planned for my future and how I react to this thing we call life.

One of the most influential figures known around the world is Rev. Dr. Martin Luther King, Jr. I identify with him because I was born at the time of his sudden death in 1968. His dream shows us that there is hope in trusting God. The realization of his dream appeared to be distant and unreachable. But his dream prevailed, and continues to carry on, reminding us that where there is God, there is hope for a better tomorrow, that there is strength in working and standing together and that loving our brothers and sisters is mandatory . He believed that dreams visualized through the grace of God, no matter how far-reaching they may seem, are attainable, and can be reached by the strength of our convictions, and our love for our fellow man.

As an adult, I am deeply saddened by the lack of kindness and compassion that people have for one another. We pass by people every day on the street, and barely notice them. I suspect, very few people could describe anything about that person. It would be as if we never saw them. Our society has adopted an "if you aren't in a position to help me, then I really don't need to get to know you," attitude. We were born to be in fellowship with one another; to develop relationships that will help one another attain our spiritual, personal and professional goals, yet most of us leave out the most important person for whom we should be in relationship with......Jesus!

He is the faceless leader of all generations from now until eternity, and without Him we would all remain a lost generation....no name and no face.

TWO

ATTITUDES AND CONFORMITY

Growing up in an all white Catholic School often times made me feel like a big lump of clay. I was unshaped and very different from everyone else. While my life mirrored many of the kids at my school, for example, having a two-parent upper middle class working family, I knew that I was set apart from everyone else and was hungry to find myself.

I have my mother to thank for my Corpus Christi Catholic School experience.
She was an English teacher who worked in public education and wanted me to have all the extra-curricular activities that public schools couldn't offer. My mother only wanted the best for me.

During my four years there, I played basketball and

ran track. I was very athletic and extremely popular. I felt important and needed. My self-esteem was high and my self-confidence was established. I felt like I was on top of the world.....until my parents decided to transfer me to a public school.

I began attending public school starting in the eighth grade at Dick Dowling Junior High School. I started the school year off with great expectations of carrying my private school popularity into my new school environment. Boy; was I wrong. While everyone looked like me, I still was set apart, but not the way I anticipated. I was the outcast of my entire 8th grade class. Although I played basketball and ran track, I was no longer the star. I rode the bench and was placed as a distance runner instead of a sprinter. Despite my challenges socially and athletically, I definitely matured a bit during my Dowling Middle School days.

From grade nine through twelve, I attended Madison High School. It was there that I had a chance to surround myself with the familiar faces of friends that I grew up with in my neighborhood. While I was happy to be among them, it didn't inspire me to perform academically. My attitude toward my school work was awful. Most of my classes were challenging and made me take on a "just forget it" type of disposition. Somewhere at this time in my life, my personality began to evolve. I began to question adult authority, lifestyle and societal choices. I trusted my parents, but I wanted to be my own person, I wanted to be able to follow the crowd if and when I felt like it!

THREE

GREAT FAMILY INFLUENCES

My parents are great role models for me. They loved one another as well as my brother and me. They both valued education and are well educated. My mom earned her Bachelors in Music and Masters of Education. My dad earned a Bachelors of Science in Pharmacy. While they worked hard at building our love for education; they worked even harder to ensure that our Christian foundation was solid.

My Christian experience began at St Benedict, a Catholic Church in Houston, Texas. My mother was the music director and my brother and I were both members of the church. At the age of thirteen, I became an altar boy at St. Benedict's.

On the days I did not serve as an altar boy, my assigned

seat was right next to my mother as she directed the choir. At times, Mass was boring to me, especially if I was not involved. I would daydream and drift off into la-la land and end up falling asleep, with my head hitting the back of the church pew. I tried to stay awake, but all that "chanting"!

Because my brother was so much older than I, he usually was assigned babysitting duty outside whenever I wanted to play. If he wanted to go out with his own friends, my Mom wouldn't let me go with him. I would get angry, and go cry in my bedroom. I wanted to go with my big brother! My mom always tried to make me feel better, by helping me get over those moods. At times, she would stop what she was doing and play cards or games with me, or she would ask me to help her prepare something for dinner. I was always eager to help her. The best part about helping mom was when she would decide to bake a cake. This was one thing I loved to do from start to finish, especially licking the batter off the beaters from the mixture. My mother had a special way of always making me feel good. She exposed me to many extracurricular activities to help me identify where I fit in. I learned how to play the piano, drums, cornet and guitar. She taught me by example how to be frugal.

My father loved to bowl, so every Saturday morning

he would take us to the bowling alley to practice with him. We actually became very good at this sport, which I still enjoy, mainly because it's something we do together.

My parents would allow me to spend the night, on occasion, at a friend's house. I thought he was pretty cool, because he drank Kool-Aid and ate Spam. At my house, we drank Coke and ate Rib Eye Steaks. I liked what my friends had and wondered why we didn't have those types of foods at our house. Like most kids, I always wanted something different than what my parents offered me.

My parents did what most parents do. They tried to uncover my talent by enrolling me in various activities from soccer to baseball, and by purchasing many musical instruments. Regardless of how well I performed and interacted in these activities, I never felt totally connected in any of them. I was frustrated. Feeling lost and scared was not a good feeling, but I understood that my parents were trying to guide me on the right path. Scripture says, (*"Train up a child in the way he should go, and when he is old he will not depart from it."*)*Proverbs 22:6.*

FOUR

MANUALLY OCCUPIED

Youth Time Clock

When I started eleventh grade, Mom said it was okay to play football. However, by then, I didn't want to, because the other kids had a head start, and performed better. Instead, I participated in ROTC drill team competitions, performed in talent shows, break dancing and "poppin'" at James Madison High School on the south side of Houston.

The Junior Navy's ROTC program is a program that prepares a person for life with discipline. After completing the junior program, I considered enlisting in the U.S. Navy; but I couldn't swim, which is a major requirement for admission.

One of my high school curriculums was a co-op program, which teaches students how to create their own personal resume and gives them the skill set to correctly complete an application for employment. There were times when we would get dismissed from school early for the purpose of working or looking for a job.

Instead, my friends and I, out of sight of grown-ups, proceeded to commit the heinous sin of smoking cigarettes and drinking. We'd blow perfect smoke rings into the air and talk about everything; including the girls that were "brickhouse" beauties. More than anything, I think we enjoyed the ritual of smoking. We considered ourselves men, not boys, and there was nothing like a good afternoon smoke to consecrate that feeling.

After graduating from high school, I felt like I was pushing my way through walking traffic. I had no idea of what lie ahead, or how I was going to get there. I took a test to join the Army because I thought this would be easy. I thought they would accept ANYONE! I failed by two points, but little did I know about the plan that God had waiting for me. *(His promises are received by faith and are given as a free gift.")* Romans 4:16. NLT

In 1986 I enrolled at ITT Technical Institute for

Electronics off of Roark Road in Houston, Texas. This was a backup plan that I had in my head for years. One of my friend's fathers was an electrician. My friend had a boom-box with thousands of blinking lights, which fascinated me. I thought if I had a degree in electronics, I could fix anything around the house that needed repairing. In the past, I had the privilege to install car stereos in automobiles, so I said, "Why not?"

I took Fundamental Math, a course that was mandatory and much needed in this field. Lab was okay, but Theory caught me off guard. The teacher wrote equations on the blackboard which was supposed to be written down. He was so quick to erase them that most of us didn't have enough time to copy the notes. I made a "B" in Lab, but had a hard time passing Theory.

One evening at school, the professor surprised us by showing the class the inside of a television. The radios I had installed in the past had six to ten wires so when the instructor opened the back panel... Uhhh... I was speechless. . . There must have been 1,000 wires....all different colors. My eyes went "BOING!!" Too much information....I was outta there!

While I was experimenting with my career choices, I was introduced to a new house of worship. In 1986, a friend invited me to Brentwood Baptist Church. I was impressed by their presentation, and no "thees" and "thous". I understood the message clearly. My parents were okay with this as long as I went to church. I quickly became a member of the Brentwood Baptist Church where I worshipped for seventeen years. In 2006 I joined The Fountain of Praise, a non-denominational church, of which I am still a member.

FIVE

THE ANGEL THAT GOD SENT

In 1987, my Grandmother's first cousin flew from Tacoma to Houston to visit my dad's mom. We called her Cousin Fannie. Boy... she was a diva and wore that title proudly, without guilt or shame. She had long, wavy, gray, silky hair. We used to tease her by asking if she was wearing a weave. She would put her hands on her hips, smile and say, "Pull it... everything that God gave me is real". She was a "DIVA"! When I say a diva, I mean she would out-dress any age group, young or old, as the light bounced off of the diamond brooch pinned on her St. John tops.

She was very engaging and could keep you smiling while depositing wisdom right into the cavity of your brain. I would just sit there and soak up every last drip of knowledge she had to offer. She was married to an honored military man, whom we called Major. I wasn't sure if that was his real name, or a nickname given because of serving so many years in the military. He was a quiet man, but very stern.

During her visit with us, she would ask me many questions, like what I was doing with my life and what my goals were? I was just a kid, and didn't know what I was going to do the next day let alone how I was going to spend the rest of my life. I felt like such a dummy. I didn't feel like I was capable of doing anything worthwhile. I told her I liked to cook, but only for a hobby, nothing more. She told me about this school, "Bates Technical College," a vocational school in Tacoma, Washington.

Upon returning to Tacoma, Cousin Fannie sent me a brochure outlining the school's curriculum.
At that same time, I had inquired about the University of Houston's Hotel and Restaurant Management curriculum. This was a popular choice among many of my friends. I decided to go out on a limb, and I enrolled into the cooking program at "Bates", in Tacoma, Washington, scheduled to begin in the fall of 1987.

See It Through My Eyes

Waking up in the city of Tacoma can be a wonderful experience of nature. The early morning sun sneaks out from behind Mount Rainier to wake up the people of this quiet town. Its' presence is never felt for very long, as rain clouds quickly appear, as if on cue… nebulous, grey and weighty, to take over for the remainder of almost each and every day. Wow, the fresh aroma of greenery flows through the air with pine trees casting their fragrance throughout the city. The streets are slick and wet as people trample on them to and from work. Tacoma is not as busy as its sister city, Seattle; which has more experience and girth to hold a brawler style of clientele.

My grandma's cousin offered to let me stay at her huge house. For the first three weeks before school started, I thought I would just enjoy my newly found freedom by drinking, going out on the town, enjoying no parental supervision.

I guess there should have been some ground rules laid regarding
 responsibilities for living with Cousin Fannie. Shortly after I moved in, she asked me to clean the exterior windows of her house. Being young and hard-headed, I gave her lip. I didn't think staying there free of charge

involved working on this big two-story "mansion." She disagreed, called my dad and reminded him she was helping me out and that I was unappreciative. She was quite upset and wanted me out!

While awaiting my dad's arrival the following week, I stayed with Cousin Fannie's daughter, Norma, who lived fifteen minutes away. Once Dad arrived, Norma and he worked quickly to find an apartment and a car for me. He didn't get on my case... he was cool... down to earth. He understood that kids are not perfect. Once I was settled, Dad flew back to Houston. Later that year, I patched things up with Cousin Fannie, and we stayed in contact until she went to be with the Lord in August, 2005.

SIX

PREPARING THE MEAL

In the few weeks I had to myself, prior to my first day of school, I was a bit nervous and apprehensive, but memories of making pizza from scratch, raisin bread and layer cakes with my mom eased my fears. Since I grew up helping in the kitchen and actually enjoyed it, I felt culinary school was probably a great fit for me.

I started attending classes at Bates, on the "new" South Campus off 78th Street and I-5. I took no summer breaks and went to school full-time. There were about twenty five students in my class.

I had two professors during that time. One took shortcuts and chewed Redman tobacco every now and then, spitting into his small cup that sat on his desk. The other was just the opposite. He had been a chef in many Las Vegas hotels. He was transferred to the old downtown location, of Bates. I begged for a transfer to study under him, and was granted the transfer. He taught multiple stations, and we worked them all: Butcher, Fry/Sauté, Pastry, Salad and Store Room. Every month we rotated stations. Part of our curriculum was to follow the daily lunch menu that was given to us by the professor.

I loved the school and studied hard. I discovered that this was the profession for me. It was my passion to watch people enjoy what was created as a masterpiece on a small dainty plate. I felt the climax of God's grace flowing through my veins. It felt very soothing as He guided me to a higher dimension of maturity.

Other students in the class were not as focused as I was. I quickly learned all stations in a short amount of time. There were many times I had to work multiple stations because of students being absent. Every time they failed to come to class, I would earn the recognition for stepping into their job without complaining. My mom always told me that, "No one owes you anything", so I kept on pushing forward into my new field of study.

Every two hours, there was a "knife drill" and everyone had to stop what they were doing. The professor would check to ensure we were holding the knife correctly, our fingers guiding the knife; and that we kept all fingers intact.

We did many challenging things while at school. The station that everybody could not wait to get to was the fry station, where you learn how to flip an egg without it splattering on the floor. We learned how to flip an egg in the pan by using a slice of toast and even though the stove often got plastered with the yolks and whites that missed the pan, it sure was a blast!

We also made ice carvings out of huge blocks of ice, using chisels, hammers, and a chain saw. We used a picture of what we wanted to carve, and stuck it against the ice. We chiseled the outline of the picture and used a chain saw to cut away the excess ice. Once the core was made, we perfected it.

I attended school five days a week, from 6:30 A.M. to 3 P.M. After school I worked at Fircrest Golf Club on Regency Blvd, five days a week from 3:30 to 9:30 P.M. I started as a prep cook and worked my way up to banquets and weddings. It was exciting to create the showy settings using mirrors as a base for cheese and fruit displays. What I really enjoyed the most about the wedding receptions was when I had the opportunity to carve a whole leg of beef. This was a huge task that challenged all of us. With two lines, one on each side of the eight -foot table, I stood at the very end, with knife in hand, ready to carve and serve. It looked like a Michael Jackson Thriller video as the people came forth, hungry, demanding to eat.

Schedule

Attending school full time and working thirty hours a week, kept my schedule quite hectic. One of my neighbors at the apartment complex, Rodriguez Keys, was a scuba diving student. One day he came over, knocked on my door and said "You never have any free time, and when you finally do get a day off, you sit in your apartment." I answered, "Yeah, it's raining". He said, "That is to be expected, we are in Washington State." I was so used to living in Houston, where, if it rained, we just stayed inside until it stopped. But in Washington State it rarely stops raining so everyone enjoys all types of outdoor activities, rain or shine. I realized I had to venture out from my comfort zone in order to explore the world outside of school and work. That took some getting used to.

A fellow student at the South Campus, by the name of D.P., had a weekend job working as a club manager at the NCO (Non-Commissioned Officers) Club in Fort Lewis. He was much older than I was. Whenever I had nights off, mostly during holidays, D.P. would ask me if I wanted to come to the NCO Club. His invitations would make me so happy because that's where the real parties were, and at no financial charge to me. But not everyone was welcome. I remember having to go through so much just to get on to the military base (log in, identification check, etc.) Since it was because of my friend that my admittance was granted, I had to pay a different price. As the manager of the club, plus bouncer at times, we had to be at the club two hours before opening and two hours after closing so he could close the books and lock the doors. It got so late in the night I would usually crash at his house until sunrise. Was it worth it? I guess it was.

My last days of school were now crawling by. My time in Tacoma, Washington was coming to a close. This was a tearful time of joy for me, a lost little boy from Houston, who had no idea how he could dominate the task of finishing anything, graduates from Bates Technical College with a Culinary Arts Degree.

SEVEN

THE GET AWAY

As my academic life in Washington State came to an end, it was time to say goodbye to old friends. This was such a sad time in my life. It took so long to find friends, and to bond with them was even more of a challenge for me. Each person had their gifting in areas that were astonishing, and to grab a piece of that was a treat. All of my friends were so nice and so unique.

One of my friends impressed me because he was driven by whatever task was put in front of him. Not only did he get it done, he always got things done his way. I did not understand how he could accomplish all he did, and look like such a mess. I mean, we both cooked at the same place, but when you looked at him, there was no need to ask what was on the menu because he was wearing it all over his chef jacket. But he was a darn good cook. It's been a while since I have talked to him, but every time I do he always seems to have just opened up another new restaurant or food outlet.

My other friend was a character. He was always cracking jokes. He was my supervisor at Fircrest Golf Club, and awesome to watch. He would put on a show by cutting vegetables and twirling his knives like he was in combat. What I really enjoyed most about him was that he showed a lot of compassion toward everyone around him. When his parents would have a gathering, he would invite me over to partake in whatever they were doing. It was so much fun. I thought my family in Houston was close-knit, with so many loved ones, but his family exceeded seventy-five people every time there was a gathering. I felt so comfortable because they treated me like I was their biological child. Sometimes I would have so much fun I would stay over until sunrise.

Time was moving fast now, and my last days in Tacoma were upon me. I began to gather together what I had left. I sold everything, including my car, which was a baby blue 1980 Datsun 210 SL station wagon. Yes, it was a family looking car, but you didn't have to worry about it getting stolen. It was never entered in a car show nor would it make the parking lot rally. But it was mine.

My last day in Tacoma arose with clear blue skies and the first rays of a melon-colored sun piercing through the clouds over Mount Rainier. I reflected over the past two years, while quietly sitting on a stool waiting for my cousins to arrive from Seattle. I closed my eyes and pondered over my recent past and how God had guided me through with His everlasting grace and how each person played their part to get me through this season.

"Knock, Knock"! "Who is it"? I asked. "It's your cousin, are you ready?" "Yep", I answered. At ten o'clock on a Wednesday morning we left Tacoma, Washington headed toward Seattle where my cousin lived. She and her husband owned a beautiful house in the hills near the Martin Luther King Exit. This was a great opportunity to bond closer with my cousins. During the two years of school I did not visit them because of my busy work and school schedules. As I think back, I barely had time to do anything for myself, but my two-year stint was worth every minute.

The next day my flight was set to leave for Houston, Texas at three o'clock P.M., and of course it was raining (I was still in Washington State!).. I hugged my cousins as they saw me off. Their faces reflected a pleasing look of satisfaction and pride for me, which made my two-year segment even more worth it.

Eight

THE WEEPING ROOM

She came early that morning showing her crown of thorns.
She whispered softly to tell her story about how she had been
robbed.
She was living lifeless telling me how her innocence had
been stolen,
That it runs through the blood line.
This is how she carried on, hiding the pain behind her tears.
I can tell she wanted to wash away those years by the sound
of her tone.

No one knows it, but my anger is violent.
I am still holding my silence not trying to burst open as I sit
in the same spot as she.
If I can just close my eyes and imagine that everything is
alright;
As I hold back my tears.

I have crossed over many oceans and I blame the in-between.
Life can wear you down, but I was not going to give up
now.
Can you imagine if she was your companion?
She even told me where to go.

After the dust had settled down, who is the blame?
"Lord, can I stand up to this faceless creature?"
I am begging for a drink.
You said if I drink the water, I will not die.
The Lord replied, "If you drink this water, you have to
drink it alone
And do what is right to see the light.
But you must ask me for direction for the road is rough".
I responded, "Yes, Yes, Yes. "Lord, the next time I see your
face,
Please stay ".

Swimming in the water of life, rewinding the ageless body,
I will never die.
"Teach me everything Lord"!
What I don't know I will ask.
No more restless nights,
But peaceful sleep.
Now that I am stronger,
I will take these dreams and make them mine.

Elliott G. Kelly

Nine

YOUTHFUL & SPICY

I came back home to live in my parent's house. It was a joy to be among them. They are the type of parents that are very understanding but still have always had "house-rules" set in stone.

At twenty-one, living at home was sometimes a challenge, especially if I stayed out after three A.M. Even though I explained to my parents that the clubs closed at two o'clock and that we liked to go out to eat after, Mom was hesitant with going along with my plan. She agreed to a compromise: I would have to be home by 2:30AM. Seriously, I truly respected her trust in me and kept a close eye on my watch for the remainder of my time in my parent's home.

One month after being home, I went to work at a

large hotel in southwest Houston. It was scary, of course, fresh out of Culinary School and on my first job. "Wow"! I thought to myself. As time went by, I began to get comfortable. Being a young graduate, making pretty decent money, I felt pretty invincible. "Why not enjoy myself", I said.

That's when things took a slight turn. "His will be done" became "My will. . . ." I did as I pleased, not caring what lie ahead. During that time of my life it was all about trying to be accepted. Social conformity and peer pressure played a key role in how I behaved. I believed that was okay at the time because I felt I was in control, but it was Satan that was taking control, and I was in serious danger.

The Spirit of Deception and Fear

When weekends came around, drinking was the norm and it was the socially acceptable thing to do with my friends and co-workers. During my time off I made decisions that were not based on sound reasoning. As years of my drinking continued, I made all of my decisions veiled under the Spirit of Deception. This Spirit made it easy for me to make terrible choices and rationalize my bad behavior. All kinds of thoughts were going on in my head, such as, "You will never change" and "You are out of control." That's when the Spirit of Fear sneaks in to attack.

The Sprit of Fear is at work when our spiritual vitality is affected. Negative fear chokes our faith, joy, peace and love. It binds, paralyzes, and weakens the Christian and softens him up for the arrival of other spirits, such as infirmity and bondage. *(For {the Spirit which} you have now received {is} not a spirit of slavery to put you once more in bondage to fear, but you have received the spirit of adoption {the Spirit producing sonship} in {the bliss of } which we cry, Abba (Father)! Father!) Romans 8:15*

In reality, negative fear is the negative "faith" of the devil. We tend to believe what the devil says, more than God's word, when we allow fear to reign in our lives. As children of God, we must not get tangled up into the deep opinions of others. We often try too hard to fit in. As one pastor said, "We spend the first thirty years of our life trying to fit in with society" when half of the time the opinion of others pushes us off the course God had already set up for us to win… because of FEAR. Fear of what people will say and fear of what they think about us.

The Bible says, *("Fearing people is a dangerous trap, but trusting the Lord means safety.") Proverbs 29:25. NLT "Do not believe every spirit, but test the spirits to see whether they are from God, because many false prophets have gone out into the world. By this you know the Spirit of God: every spirit that confesses that Jesus Christ has come in the flesh is from*

God; and every spirit that does not confess Jesus is not from God; this is the spirit of the antichrist, of which you have heard that it is coming, and now it is already in the world."
1 John 4:1-3. NASB

Ten

RELEASING THE TENSION

Throughout my childhood I had a rough time because of my timidness. When it came to dating, that was the hardest game to play. I felt as if I was given the instruction manual for a different game. Of course that made me a little disappointed in myself, and more depressed. I asked myself, "What must I do to find a mate"? And the more I thought about it the more frustrated I became. I can remember when I told myself that I would probably be the last person in the world to get married.

Well, that almost happened, until a beautiful young lady crossed my path in the year of 1995. Wow! She was a knockout; very spontaneous and a lot of fun. She had caramel colored skin, long silky hair and a beautiful figure. I met her, my future wife, while attending a party at a friend's house. She was dating someone else, but was ending the relationship. We dated for two very happy years before getting married. Unfortunately, as the years went by, our differences in personality and interests became quite apparent and put great distance between us. We began to live separate lives as I began to rub my pain with alcohol daily.

Eleven

WEAPONS OF WARFARE

After seven years of marriage, I thought nothing could be worse than losing the one I loved. Yes, I was separated from my wife at the time. Not knowing what to do, I still seemed to go through life numbing myself day after day. Searching after the wrong thing, feeling sorry for myself, I was looking for a pity party. I found myself drifting to the house of Lucifer, where Satan dwells. I was unguarded and my soul was weakened by the many bites that the demons had put in me.

Months went by and my adversary was consuming me, physically and spiritually. I found myself not caring about the future. My daily life was haunted by demons. Listening to their conversation and schemes of what they were going to do to me, I just sat there not knowing who was on my side. My friends stopped calling. My phone stopped ringing. Several times I picked up the phone to see if it was working; not understanding what was taking place.

After a period of time, it didn't take as long to get drunk. My tank was half full all the time. After a few drinks, I would start calling everyone in my address book, and talk about anything that came to mind. The next day, I had forgotten the conversation, and would ask a person about something I had just talked about the previous evening, which caused some raised eyebrows.

One Friday night I came home to watch television and started hearing weird noises. I immediately turned the TV off and looked over my shoulder. There I saw the devil, big and dark with curly hair on his head, chest, and arms. He had large, sharp eyes and two fangs. His voice was more of a deep, echoing sound than actual words. I escaped his presence by running through the house, grabbing clothes to wear the next day, because I was not going to stay there that night. I got in my truck and sped off to the nearest hotel, a Holiday Inn off of Highway 59, thirty-five minutes from my house.

TWELVE

THE FINAL ROUND

Frazzled and exhausted by what had just happened, the Lord laid me down to rest and was coaching me step by step for the battle to come. Through the power of the Holy Spirit, God told me to tighten my breastplate and be prepared to take position. So, I did. When sunrise came, I woke up with a Champion Anointing. It reminded me of a boxer getting pumped up to meet his opponent before entering the ring.

As I left the hotel and drove back home, I felt this boldness come over me which I had never felt before. When I drove up to my house, I felt an imaginary crowd of demons from the dark world cheering on their leader, the devil. Then the Holy Spirit began to give me instructions, saying, "Go into the house and open the front door, back door and find some olive oil." It was not me doing this, but the Holy Spirit guiding me.

He said, "Walk through your house and where I tell you to scatter the oil, you do so." I said, "Yes I will obey." As I was doing what the Holy Spirit said, I was raging all through the house flinging oil all over the walls and then I began to pray in the Spirit.

This went on for an hour after a tiring battle with the monster that had controlled my past. Thereafter, a fresh wind passed through the house and God said, "It is over, rest in peace". *(God blesses those who mourn, for they will be comforted.) Matthew 5:4.NASB*

Meeting the Great "I Am"

I had just experienced the greatest moment in my life. Dialoguing with the Father one-on-one, I had a better understanding of who God is and what His Kingdom is actually all about. I could now understand prophecies in a much better way and now knew what to do with them when I received them.

Intimacy is what God wants. I remember hearing once that Intimacy means, "Knowing each other's heart without limitation and sharing each other's heart without reservation." If we talk with God, He will share His heart with us.

You are probably asking yourself how do you talk to God? The answer is, just like you do when you talk to another person. And you do not have to scream. God is not deaf. He already knows what you are going through. He is just waiting for you to come to Him.

Thirteen

THY KINGDOM COME

I suddenly heard a whisper in my ear saying, "Dust yourself off and walk into your Destiny." As I looked back at my life, I saw all of the clutter and confusion. I gazed into the prophetic lenses. I saw myself walking on golden bricks, dressed in a white cloak and sitting on a throne in the higher places.

Then "Bam!" revelation hit me all at once. "You are a King." The Hebrew word for King is 'melekh' which means to possess, to reign' and that's what I felt. The Lord had separated me from my foes right before my eyes and had given me the name "King" to reign over any adversary that was to come my way.

From that moment on I began letting go of the baggage I was holding on to and began Spiritual

House Cleaning. I replaced everything from carpeted floors to tile and bedding. Old picture frames came off the walls and were replaced with The Ten Commandments. Worldly magazines were replaced with Bible Commentaries.

Then the Lord told me to burn Hyssop fragrance candles in the house for a whole week. Hyssop represents the image of spiritual cleansing from sin. Not understanding what I was doing, I was still guided by the Holy Spirit to be obedient and to follow orders, for the Lord is RIGHTEOUS.

Today, it still blows my mind, not knowing what had taken place. The Lord guided my footsteps through the instructions of the Holy Spirit. As I went through a transformation, so did my house. Now it is my home where I reign, which I call the "King's Palace". It is my sanctuary and a resting place.

The Gift of Discernment

Discerning of Spirits refers to the God-given ability to tell whether a prophetic speech came from God's Spirit or from another source opposed to God. Some people think this gift is only good in a church setting or an evangelistic meeting. But this gift will help you discern evil from good no matter where you are. It can save you from destruction.

You will know when to run and when to stand still. I like to think of discernment as a tool that triggers the Holy Spirit. They work hand-in-hand as a team. In the next paragraphs I will share my personal experiences on how discernment guided me throughout my journey. *("The mind of the intelligent seeks knowledge, But the mouths of fools feeds on folly".) Proverbs 15:14.*

The Devils Playground Experience

It was only a few years ago that I stumbled upon the playground of the enemy. Come with me as the Lord shows me the manifestation of the Devil and his scandalous ways.

The Following are some of the unforgettable times that I have been Miraculously Used by the Power of God and to be His Anointed Witness:

(1) One evening after work I took the same way home as usual. I entered my neighborhood with ease. Suddenly I felt a nudge in my Spirit telling me not to go home just yet. I had sensed a disturbance on my street. I did as the Holy Spirit commanded and I took an alternate route. When I finally arrived home there were two ambulances on my street. I

walked across to my neighbor's house and asked what had happened. He said a shooting had just taken place.

(2) I was in my hotel room one Friday night in Baton Rouge, taking part in a Bowling Tournament when the phone rang. "Do you want to go to the casino?" my teammate asked me. "Sure why not, it beats staying in the hotel," I answered back. There was a group of us anticipating a showdown at the casino. We walked outside of the lobby and the bus pulled up. We all got on the bus, and then suddenly the Spirit of God hovered over me. It was like floating in and out of Heaven and Earth.

As we entered the casino grounds, the Lord showed me railroad tracks that stretched across just before the entrance of the parking lot. I did not know why the Lord was showing me this, but I knew that the spirit of the Holy Ghost was with me; very much alive and active.

We all got off the bus, and a large group ahead of me entered the double glass doors of the casino. When we entered, I noticed there were steep steps at the right inside of the casino. Since metamorphosis was taking place; the Holy Spirit became very sensitive. I began to go down the steep stairway toward the gateway of the casino.

Suddenly, I felt a strong sickness coming over me. I began to feel nauseated as my head began to spin rapidly. I rushed up the stairs to find a place to sit down. Then the Lord spoke, "I am the one that kicked him out of Heaven. Satan did not want to listen to what I had to say. So, he resides here".

I went outside for some fresh air and the Lord was showing me the Devil orchestrating his demons to invite the guests in with a greeting smile. I was astonished as I watched all of this go on. I continued to monitor this activity for three hours. I sat until the people that I came with were ready to go back to the hotel. Boy! I was ready to leave that place.

When the bus pulled up I hurried on and sat down pondering what I had just witnessed. I sat there separating myself from the noise and suddenly my ears were filled with worship music. It was like I was the only person that could hear the music.

There was a long line to exit the casino parking lot. Car loads were pulling in one by one as I cried out in silence. "Go back, go back," I wanted to say. Still waiting in line for over thirty minutes, out of nowhere a train crossed in front of the casino and blocked the entrance and exit way of the casino. I thought to myself that this has got to be the longest train ever. It kept coming as if it had no end to it.

Twenty minutes passed by and I noticed the cars in front of us began to get out of line to drive back to the casino. Again the Lord was showing me another demonstration of the Devil. The train was used to frustrate the people so they would go back into the devil's pit, the casino. It was like a police officer controlling the traffic light during peak business hours.

After being in line for over thirty minutes the crossbar gate raised and we drove out of the parking lot. I looked back and started to cry in silence as innocent victims entered the casino to nourish their souls.

(3) On another bowling trip heading to Dallas, Texas, my father and I had made several rest stops but this next stop had my Spirit moving with caution. As my father pulled up behind a tractor-trailer, I told him I felt that this trailer was going to back up into our vehicle. He stated, that "He should be able to see that we are parked behind him." I tried to convince my father, but his mind was set on not moving. When we came back from the restroom my Spirit was discerning that our vehicle had been hit. As we turned the corner my father could not believe what had just happened. I tried

to explain but he was still in unbelief of what had just happen.

(4) On that same trip, after I had checked into this hotel I saw one of my bowling teammates in the lobby. We walked outside to talk and a stranded young woman approached us. She asked us if we would help her by giving her $5.00 dollars for gas because her tank was on empty. My teammate responded with hopelessness. I told him to take the stranded woman to the gas station and buy her gas. Because of the strong anointing that had been hovering over me, I was very confident to follow through with God's plan. Plus I told my teammate that he will be paid back in triple. So, when he returned from getting the gas for her, he told me the salesperson gave him a FREE gas container for the fuel. The next day at the bowling tournament, my teammate won $300.00 dollars for bowling a great series of high scoring games. Go figure; I think it was the Grace of God for him being obedient to our Lord.

(5) One Wednesday evening I was on the phone with a friend's mother. She was telling me how busy her week had been. She told me that she misplaced $20.00 dollars and that she had been trying to locate it for several hours. Immediately the Lord

showed me that the $20.00 dollars was in the left pocket of a coat she had worn to church, and it was hanging in her closet. She was shocked when she reached into her church-coat pocket and pulled out the twenty dollar bill.

Many times our conscience will notify us of what's going on around us, but we have to be in tune with it. I call this the Holy Spirit signaling us to take action. He lives inside all of us so we have to believe what He is saying and showing us.

So, a mindset of unbelief will taint all we do. For some people, no matter what God says; His Word will be filtered through a grid of unbelief and will keep them trapped in the wilderness and going in circles.

So, can you hear God's voice? Yes, very much so. Just as He spoke to Moses in the burning bush, He can still speak through you as He did through me.

FOURTEEN

WHY GOD DISGUISES HIS PRESENCE

The New Testament talks about Jesus ascending into heaven. But, right before he was ascended into heaven, He gave the disciples a command to preach the Good News all over the world. Jesus said that He will be with us in the Spirit and as believers we are called to be servants to Christ. It also mentions that older men are to teach younger men and older women are to teach younger women, passing along His message from one generation to another.

I call God's messengers, "Ministering Angels". Throughout my life I have been deeply touched by Ministering Angels. As I think back to the beginning of my transformation, my first Ministering Angel was a friend, who understood exactly what I was going through because she was going through a transformation herself. We both were running to Christ with teary eyes.

The Second Ministering Angel took me out of my comfort zone, which was the worldly ways, and pulled me behind the veil of worship. It was like I was touring Heaven. As I began to submerge myself, I started to ask questions about eternity, my Heavenly Father and the purpose of my life. Instruction was being downloaded from the Ministering Angel to me and I was consumed with A Holy Impartation.

The Third Ministering Angel was a woman who took me under her wing and pushed me onto the battlefield. She had been in the ministry for more than twenty years and stretched my faith by asking me to pray in front of small groups. I was so scared, not knowing what to say or how to pray. She also asked me to partake in Christian Conferences held in different cities in the state of Texas. I felt that if I had said no, I would have disappointed God. But I knew this was His plan, so I chose to be obedient and follow His direction. Within a year's time, God had pushed me through multiple Christian conferences and classes. It felt like I was getting private lessons from God, Himself.

FIFTEEN

CAN YOU HEAR MY CRY?

As His children, we think we must be unpredictable to God. But just as an earthly father, He is around us enough to know our patterns and our ways. God is always interested in our daily concerns but He also knows the temptations of the world. We often want God to see only the good side of us, like helping an elderly woman cross the street, but we do not want God to see us committing the harsh sins we perform on a daily basis, such as not telling the truth to a parent or indulging in adultery or fornication. The truth is, God is everywhere and He sees everything.

Some ask why God gives us choices. Well, that's simple. Would I like someone to dictate my every move? I think my answer would probably be NO! So, God gives us the freedom to make our own choices in life. Time and time again He is watching us go through all of this so we will get tired of worshiping worldly things and perhaps begin to worship Him. There are only two roads we can take and that is God's way into the Heavenly places or the Darkness of the pit of Hell where the devil resides.

When we are born into this world, we are innocent babies ..... Then the world that's full of sin attaches to us in a magnetic way. From that point on it's our job to ask Jesus to come into our heart so we may be saved.

Spirit of Bondage

With peer pressure being the norm, often times, we are fooled by demonic spirits disguised as friends. I myself was a victim of this spirit of bondage.

Without realizing it, I had allowed my nicotine and alcohol addiction to consume me. It's just like opening the door when the doorbell rings. You are basically saying "Come on in, make yourself at home." And we know what that means. This addiction became a stronghold; which is anything that holds onto you without coming off easily.

So, I tried to turn this addiction over to God. I was

hoping that He would understand. Well, He didn't. The Lord said to me, "This is not a disease, this is a desire." First, I had to recognize where my help comes from, which is our Savior, Jesus. If you don't know your rights as a child of God, how can you defend yourself?

For over twenty years I was feeling sorry for myself, thinking I was not going to overcome this predicament. I also thought this was the end of the road; meaning, I was going to be like this for the rest of my life. I did not care about living or trying to better my life. See, the enemy wants us to be content with the situation we are in, not what we can become.

We think God is going to take care of everything while we sit and wait. But we must do our part. We must seek His Glory. He will guide us, but we have to choose the right path ourselves, not sit around on our butts. For years I cried to myself and wondered why I was living like I was. I tried over and over to quit this alcohol addiction on my own and with my own power and will, but could not manage to succeed.

It was Saturday, the second of September, 2006, when a miraculous thing happened to me. While smoking a cigarette and drinking a cocktail, I sat down on a chair, in my garage, bent over, put my head between my hands and began to cry. With tears coming down my

face shaking my head side to side, I said, "I'm tired."
I screamed out, "JESUS!" Within a flash of a second,
an audible voice came in my ear saying, "IT'S OVER."
Immediately I discarded both addictions. Later that
day I asked Jesus, "Did you not hear my cry or was
it not loud enough?" Jesus replied, "I saw you and I
heard your cry, but you did not call me by NAME."

*"I tell you the truth, anyone who believes in me will do the
same works I have done, and even greater works, because I am
going to be with the Father. You can ask for anything in my
name, and I will do it, so that the Son can bring glory to the
Father. Yes, ask me for anything in my name, and I will do
it!" John 14:12-14 NLT*

SIXTEEN

RECOVERY FROM INTENSIVE CARE

At that time in my life, I felt like I was undergoing "spiritual surgery." I was under God's microscope so He could get a closer look at all the sin I had put on through my life's journey. As He began to cut, I began to bleed. The pain was so severe; I couldn't wait until He was done. The "surgery" was lengthy but well worth it.

As God began to shape and mold me, I asked Him "Why are you doing this? Am I worth it?" God said, "I sent my son Jesus to show you the way of life and you submitted yourself to Him. As you showed your passion and love to Jesus, so you have shown your passion and love toward Me." After that moment I was a little overwhelmed because I had never felt so much love before.

Then Jesus showed me a picture of Himself hanging on a tree in Calvary, and it dawned on me that He hung on a tree bleeding just for me. So, I prostrated my face to the floor worshiping Jesus as I wept. Then Jesus said, "IT IS FINISHED, IT'S ALL OVER, no more shame, no more disease, no more loneliness, no more rejection, no more death, only life because of Me. Now heaven comes to earth and the dead are living. Now the unwanted are chosen."

I asked Jesus, "What do I do with such a gift? What do I do with such a mystery? Can I be an open door to your love? Make me a friend to the rejected ones. Let me be a safe place for the people who feel endangered."

The next day I prayed, thanking God for all his wonderful works until I fell into a deep sleep. When I woke up, I looked in the mirror, and noticed that I was a new creature who had been operated on through a spiritual rebirth.

So in order to birth newness, I had to leave past issues in the past and I relied on the new ones that God had birthed in me. This was a time to let go. . .

Sometimes we hold onto the past because we believe there is something we still need. We cling to certain things because we fear we'll never be able to replace them. No, God has more in store for us. If you've entrusted your future in Him you haven't seen your best days yet. There's more ahead for you than behind you. A friend told me, "The front windshield view is wider than the rear view mirror," meaning when you look in the rear view mirror, the view is narrow. So, why look back when the future of opportunity in front of you is much broader.

So with God's strength, get up, get over it and move on to what He has called you to do.

Here are three scriptures to get you started in the right direction:

1. *Instead, be kind to each other, compassionate, tenderhearted, forgiving each other, just as God through Christ has forgiven you. Ephesians 4:32.NLT*

2. *No, dear brothers and sisters, I have not achieved it, but I focus on this one thing: forgetting the past and looking forward to what lies ahead, I press on to reach the end of the race and receive the heavenly prize for which God, through Christ Jesus, is calling us. Philippians 3:13-14. NLT*

3. *I, even I, He Who blots out and cancels your transgressions,*

for My own sake, and I will not remember your sins.
Isaiah 43:25.AMP

Transformed By Truth

If you know the story about Saul's Conversion, then we know it is one of the most remarkable testimonies in the Bible. Saul, now named Paul, was transformed into one of the greatest Apostles of all time. The story has a great impact on me because I could really relate to his blindness of not knowing God and the timing of God's hand. After being flipped and tossed and molded, I am still amazed at the vitality in my heart. I went before God because I was sick and God performed the greatest miracle of all: the re-birth of human flesh. It is the most spectacular gift to mankind. It does not come free; this gift comes with a hefty price tag on it.

In my pursuit of God, I lost close friends and loved ones. At first I did not understand why I was so lonely and why no one wanted to come around. Then it finally dawned on me that God was blocking the disturbance so I would give Him the full attention He deserves. He had me sit in silence most of the time while He showed me His purpose. It felt like the room was spinning and I could not move until the sprinkling of God's Anointing was finished. It felt like God was telling me the mysteries of the Kingdom.

He showed me I was never alone in any situation. He also shared with me the hearts of people. He showed me that everybody was hurting and suffering, dying slowly because of the hidden traps put down by Lucifer, the adversary. God showed me that my life plays a major part of the big picture. He uses all of us to play a part for His story.

Remember the things I have done in the past. For I alone am God! I am God, and there is none like me. Only I can tell you the future before it even happens. Everything I plan will come to pass, for I do whatever I wish. I will call a swift bird a prey from the east- a leader from a distant land to come and do my bidding. I have said what I will do, and I will do it. Isaiah 46:9-11.

When God has an objective, He seeks out a man or a woman to fulfill His purpose. Utilizing both the positive and negative circumstances of life, God molds and shapes individuals toward the fulfillment of their destiny.

This was actually the beginning of the journey. God's anointing was so heavy that my negatives became my positives. Because I didn't smile much, I was often told that I was a hard person to approach. Holding the temperament of melancholy, I was always sad and felt that life was so unfair to me.

God said, "Pour out what I have poured into you." So, I did. God guided me in encouraging others that everything was going to work out according to His plan. Serving God's people was my first assignment. I have been an ear piece to many who have cried on my shoulder, knowing that the only way they could trust me was to see the shining light within me. That was God working within me.

The more I blessed others, the more God blessed me. I remember when I first started tithing, in accordance with God's will, I was shown a miracle!

The money miracle happened when I went to the bank to cash a check and was so scared to see the balance because of tithing. God deposited $2000.00 dollars in my checking account. I just knew that my balance was under $200.00 dollars. I checked it several times! Now, I tithe faithfully, not because of what He did, but because it is His will.

SEVENTEEN

INTIMATE WORSHIP

V. Michael McKay, a legendary song writer was my mentor in becoming a born-again Christian.

I was introduced to V. Michael through a friend at church. He was the choir director at Brentwood Baptist Church.One day we had a talk. I was looking for a spiritual advisor. He answered so many of my basic questions about the Bible and what the scriptures meant. What's a Pharisee? What's a Sadducee? What was their importance? What was their significance?

He invited me to his house, and I thought to myself, WOW! As I browsed through his home, I noticed multiple plaques of recognition in the music industry of worship.

He had a big piano in the living area. While I was there the doorbell rang and fifteen women walked in. I was pulled into another world when he sat at the piano, started playing, and the women started worshipping with songs of praise.

He encouraged me in many different ways, through his uplifting words and his music. Now that my life has turned around, I no longer need his daily intervention, but continue to enjoy his friendship in Christ.

EIGHTEEN

UNDERSTANDING PROPHECY

Prophecy is a gift from the Holy Spirit. Anybody can prophesy provided he is a born-again believer, filled with the Holy Spirit and open to moving in the supernatural.

When I first understood that prophecy is a God-given tool to encourage others and edify myself, it was so new to me; it was like I was floating on cloud nine. The dialogue was so clear between God and me. To move in the prophetic gift you need to remain open to hearing Gods voice. Prophetic words have different strengths of impact depending on the situation, circumstance and faith level of the receiver, as well as on the ability, experience, understanding and relationship of the giver to the Holy Spirit.

I always tell others that the entire Bible is a book of prophecy. It tells about the coming one, who is our Lord and Savior, Christ Jesus. The phrase, "The coming one" talks about the past, present and future. Prophecy also opens our eyes and mind to the way God loves and cares for us. Prophecy enables us to come to our senses and escape the possibility of being snared in the entrapment of the devil.

Prophecy can bring correction and warning. Many times the Bible talks about prophecy given to the people so they can turn from their wicked ways and repent.

Prophecy can also provide direction in a person's life so they can avoid the extra hassle of being corrupted by wrongdoings.

Prophecy is a faith injection. It changes the atmosphere in our spiritual lives and opens doors to miracles.

People flow in the prophetic differently. Some have the ears to hear from the Lord and the message will be transmitted to the one who he is receiving. Others get pictures downloaded from the Lord. When the Lord downloads these pictures to me, it's like a Polaroid camera. It's an instant picture downloaded into the visionary mind.

There have been countless times I prophesied over someone's life because the Lord either showed me that the pathway they were on was harmful, dangerous or hurtful, or that He was pleased with what they were doing and wanted to say " Well done, my faithful servant."

Remember, everyone can prophesy. It is in our DNA. We are made in God's image. It can also be abused. Giving out self-prophecy without God's guidance can injure a person's life and turn it into turmoil. Prophecy is a part of God's business, not our business. So do not speak until you have been spoken to from the Lord.

NINETEEN

REPOSSESSION OF TERRITORY

Before coming to Christ, my world was stricken at times by my stubborn behavior. I thought the money I had accumulated was ruler of all. I bought whatever I wanted at any time. I acted so foolishly that at times I thought I could even buy friendship.

I was so selfish, that my only motive for being kind to others was to see what I could get from the relationship. I was a taker! If any of those poeple ever asked something from me I would typically tell them, "No," because I was thinking only of myself. I had many nice gifts and I wasn't hurting for anything materially, but neither was I willing to give anything of myself unless it benefited ME.

Now that I am older I have become more compassionate

toward others. I understand that people need people in order to survive this life's test we are living in. It all makes so much sense that God uses people to minister to others, to make them aware of Who He is.

God's mighty hand nurtures all of us. He is our Father who sits on high looking down, encouraging us to make the right decisions in life.

In this world, we learn that many things bring destruction to our lives. Some people ask, "If God loved us why would He let us get into all this mess?" God loves us so much that He deliberately gives us a choice. And the choice is ours to make. What if you were told everything to do, or live in a country where someone else made all your choices? You would not be too happy, would you? So, *Everything He does is just and fair. "…He is a faithful God who does no wrong; how just and upright He is." Deuteronomy 32:4. NLT*

Fig Leaves

There are false coverings called "Fig Leaves." Fig leaves represent the clothing of the "false-self". We all have varying levels of fig leaves covering our lives. The fig leaves are there to cover up our nakedness. It covers up our true pain, which dwells inside of us. The purpose of pain is meant to signal something is wrong and it is also a signal to ask God for His help.

When I gave myself fully over to God, I began to ask Him to show me who I am. Although I thought my birth did not matter, God says, we are neither an accident nor a mistake. Whether or not your parents planned your birth, God did. Long before my parents conceived me, I was conceived in the mind of God.

After God showed me who I was, I asked Him to show me who the Devil is. God showed me that this creature is an invisible spirit with a hidden agenda to roam the earth to kill and destroy God's children. After this truth was revealed, I was agitated and very angry. For me to see the statue of the enemy and how it had defeated me in my body, soul and spirit, I was ready for Spiritual Warfare.

In order for me to recover my territory, I had to get serious about becoming more Christ-like and to depend on His Spirit to help me gain back what was temporarily stolen. How I executed my Christ –like actions played a major part in how successful I was at helping myself and helping and influencing others. I had to be willing to do things for the Lord. When I was doing it grudgingly, it didn't work for the Lord or me.

It all started with taking responsibility for my own shortcomings. I could sit there and blame it on someone else, but it was no one's fault but my own. Because of the choices I made, I had to prioritize my life all over again. I had to start with God as the head of every situation I put myself in, every question I asked and the motive behind every decision I made. I asked God to remove everything in my life that was not good for me even if it was going to hurt me. Of course, with some physical things, I had to remove and replace them with new items and activities. Some old habits that needed to be broken were:

*Smoking: It was destroying my inner man and my internal organs. Now I am free of the internal pollutants that were blocking my physical health and I am now exercising the temple that God blessed me with.

*Selfishness: Before my re-birth, I never gave away any of my professional services without compensation; but now I freely donate to several charities and worthy causes.

* Insecurities: I used to be shy and kept my thoughts and feelings to myself, but now, I boldly step up and encourage others to finish the race they have started.

TWENTY

POLISHING THE ARROW AND BEING EQUIPPED

Being equipped means being ready for war at anytime. For many Christians this is a new concept. Many of us think about how to take down the devil and search for tactics to bring God's children closer to Him. We, ourselves, have to be good students of the spirit that guides us, but God is calling us to do more.

Taking authority, overcoming a threat, invading territory or conquering an enemy is very dangerous if you are not trained in the righteousness of truth. It's like an army that goes to boot camp to train his or her body and to learn the different tactics to prepare for the upcoming battle. This is the same training that we Christians have to come to partake in when getting ready for Jesus' return.

Our understanding needs to expand. Jesus said, "He will never leave us, nor forsake us." So, Jesus lives in all of us to give us direction and discipline. Now, we have to be quiet and listen to what He is saying to us. Many times He speaks constantly through His word. That means you have to pick up the Bible and do some reading for yourself.

We first must pull God out of the box. Yes, the box that we put Him in. God is love, but he also carries a wrath. Wrath is a fierce anger or punishment for sins. A lot of us think God is going to brush off our sins over and over without any consequences. Here is one example of His wrath: "...*Jesus went into the temple and began to drive out those who bought and sold in the temple, and over turned the tables of the money changers and the seats of those who dealt in doves, and would not allow anyone to carry any household equipment through the temple courts. Mark 11:15-16.* AMP As you read, listen for God's voice. You will be encouraged to learn what happens both in the heavens and on earth as the two realms unfold simultaneously.

In my personal journey, He downloads different material into my storage bank. He also places me in the audience and speaks to me about what chaos has taken place and what needs to be done. It's like looking at a play on stage and seeing all that goes on and wondering how the script can be edited.

The training before going on the field is vital. You can easily get injured if you have not prepared yourself for battle.

After all of the conferences, prophetic classes and dream interpretations there will always be more to learn. Be aware, the devil is not sitting still. He is in class also.

No one knows all except for the True Living God, Jesus the Omniscience One.

TWENTY-ONE

MARRIED TO A STRANGER

Falling in love with a stranger is quite an experience. So, the question is: How often do we fall in love with someone whom we have never met? Not often, probably never. In order to fall in love with someone, you have to spend quality time together. You have to get intimate with one another. You have to know each other's heart without limitation and share each other's heart without reservation. We both know it takes time to get to this point.

In life relationships, we first have to meet someone. Then we become acquaintances. Now, if you want to invest into the relationship, you become friends. If you want to take it further, you become close friends and then best friends. Now you are at a point of opening your heart to one another and fully trusting each other with private issues that go on within yourself.

These are the same steps it takes to get intimate with the Lord, Jesus Christ, but somehow people think it's different. People often ask me, how do you talk to Jesus? I tell them I talk to Jesus just like talking to my best friend. Just think back, when you had to talk to your best friend about a matter. You would find a private place where you could talk. You would spill all of your emotions out verbally and expect your best friend to listen, without interrupting and to have your best interest at hand. It's the same principle when talking with the Lord.

In order to hear from God, you have to talk to Him and walk with Him daily. Then there is a shift in the dialogue. You will begin to recognize the voice of the Lord. This is very crucial. Lucifer, your adversary, will be upset because you are not his friend, so he will confuse you with his voice by trying to imitate the voice of the Lord. That's why it is very important to communicate with God daily. Even if you hear thousands of voices in your ear, you will be able to recognize God's voice clearly; even if it comes in a soft whisper.

In my personal life I did not appreciate the value of friendship much, because I thought I had it all. Once,

I thought I did not need anybody, but I had also been so down, thinking that no one in my life needed me. I even thought material things could fix the way I felt, but it did not.

Then I found myself all alone, a lonely man with nothing to share. I was a man with no direction and no one to love me for myself. I spent many days being alone not knowing His plan or the purpose for my life. Then one day I began to seek His face knowing He was trying to pull me up from the darkness, but my hand was clenched. When I decided to unclench my hand, He reached down and pulled me up and rocked me in His arms saying, "Everything is going to be okay."

Unconditional love is the best love a person can experience. It means there are no limits. Finally, for the first time I can be myself, without being affected by the judgment of others. Truly, no one has had all of me until now. Knowing the Truth, I can give my all to Him. The Lord has given me liberty to go all the way into my destiny. Every day is a brand new day with grace sufficiently supplied by His love. The best thing about this is I don't have to run away and hide behind the true me. I don't have to fake it, lie or pretend anymore, because of who He is, my lover of my life, Jesus Christ.

81

TWENTY-TWO

DESIGNED FOR YOU

How we define our lives determines our destiny. Destiny is defined as a predetermined course of events. It is very vital for us to understand why we are here. If we can only get an understanding of who God really is, then we will have a better reading of His purpose for our lives.

So many of us live dangerously, not knowing the plan He has already invested in us. The Bible says, "Know where you are headed, and you will stay on solid ground." Living life on purpose is the most enjoyable way to live. In order to live life on purpose, we have to know who we are. Then you have to understand that what we do in life really matters and that it has an impact on others. So, whatever we do, do it with a purpose attached to it. If there is nothing attached to it, then we are living a dangerous life headed for destruction. It is very easy to get distracted by what everybody is doing, but purpose has a purpose.

Foremost, we have to love ourselves and have dignity. If we don't love ourselves, how can we expect others to love us? Knowing yourself begins with understanding what your name means. Take time to find out the definition of your name. Yes, God already knew what our parents were going to name us before we were born. God Himself designed a plan and purpose for us, and one in which we could be guaranteed success.

A lot of people do not know this, but God intended us to be His chosen one to win. God has prepared us in advance to walk into victory. His purpose will explain to us why, and the destiny will explain where your purpose is leading you.

If you remember in the Old Testament, God used Moses to speak, as His voice to guide the Israelites into the Promised Land. In the Bible, you might see the word "seer" or "prophet". A seer or prophet is a person who speaks for God…under divine guidance, an interpreter of God's will. So, quite naturally God is doing the same works now as He did then, and He still uses us to help each other. We have to be alert and have the mindset of Christ to understand where God is taking us.

TWENTY THREE

OUR AMAZING GOD

Our God is so amazing for a multitude of reasons. First, He is Omni-present, which means, He is everywhere at the same time. He is a forgiving God who washes his memory clean of all our wrong doings. He is Love, for He loves the sinner as well as the saved!
However, adversaries always arise as if He doesn't exist.

Since God is the judge of all, we need to have a grateful attitude and life style of Godliness. Where there is no sin there is no wrath. Acknowledging and practicing a Godly lifestyle will be rewarded. Ultimately the purpose of human existence is to live before the great and glorious God in adoration, love and praise and to find Him alone in our daily walk.

The Presence of God

The presence of God's grace is such a blessing to me.

I have come to thank Jesus my Lord and Savior for the sacrifice He paid for all of us. The beating and the torture He endured showed me how to act or not act in any challenging or confrontational situation I may find myself in.

When Jesus died on the cross for our sins, He gave us power through the Holy Spirit to renounce the evil in our lives and to replace all badness with His goodness. We are given a new opportunity every day to change some things about ourselves.

When I discovered the true meaning of grace, I wanted to change everything about me that was not good in the eyes God. There is an old saying, in order to have something new you have to be willing to let go of the old. So, I put away my old habits which were crippling my life, and replaced them with His word and His goodness which rehabilitated and revitalized me.

We are all Kings and Queens of the most high so it is important for us to live responsibly and in accordance with Holy Scripture. The Bible says He is with us all the time, so why would you want to embarrass Jesus and ask for his forgiveness over and over? Just as Peter denied Christ three times, how many times are we going to deny Him?

We were chosen for this time, this era, so why waste God's grace and time by our repetitious indecisiveness and destruction?

I have come to realize that every day is a gift from God. I am often reminded through the Holy Spirit that I asked for change and it makes me want to encourage others to strengthen their faith and to trust God to change their hearts. Of course, for me this came in time and through my own self-examination. It took a lot of letting go and allowing God to have control of the situation.

A lot of us are so surrounded by chaos that we do not take the time to hear what God is saying. We want the blessing without the testing. But if we take the time to listen to what God says, we will be amazed at what He is telling us.

Today, I am living like a Royal King, cloaked in diamonds and pearls. Not, of course in the material sense but in the spiritual sense of my existence. This purpose will extend far beyond the few years you will spend on earth. God has allowed you to be here at this time in history to fulfill His special purpose for this generation. Don't be afraid. He said, "I will never leave you, nor forsake you." God is faithful to His words. Trust Him. I do!

TWENTY-FOUR

DISCOVERING THE TRUTH

Sitting outside by the river,
It was quiet and the wind was still.
I had time to think about nature's surroundings.
It's uncanny, when a person is alone,
The Teacher begins to speak.

Suddenly I glanced into the water
And His face appeared under the ripples.
I saw the will of the warrior looking directly into my eyes.
I started to question,
Searching the moment,
As my life began circling in one spot.

I asked, "What makes us chance worthy?

Then my eyes closed with tears racing for joy;

Understanding the news that was given . . .

AS

      I

            BEGAN

                    TO

                         PRAY.

When I opened my eyes everything changed under the sun.
My hunger was truly blessed by Jesus, Himself.
My sacrifice was redemption to this other place from where I
wanted to escape.

Since God is true . . .

SO

      IS

            HIS

                  WORD. . . .

Elliott G. Kelly

Words of Wisdom
FROM
THE AWAITED JOURNEY
Anticipation~Anticipating

Await-To be ready or waiting for

Await-To wait for

Journey-traveling from one place to another, usually taking a long time; to make a journey

Ready-prepared for action or use; not hesitant, willing; prompt s in comprehending

Ready-showing skills or dexterity; a ready wit; incline, dispose

Wit-to know

Dispose- to give attendancy; incline

Ready-likely at any moment

THE AWAITED JOURNEY

Ready-immediately available for use;
to make ready; prepare

Willing-dispose or consenting; incline;
cheerful consenting or ready

Willing-done; given, borne or use
with a cheerful readiness

Prompt-done; performed, delivered, without delay; quick
to act or respond; punctual; induce to action

Prompt-to give rise to or inspire;
to give a cue to; remind

Comprehending-to understand; to include; comprise

Comprise- to include or a contain;
to consist of; to form or constitute

Dexterity-skill or adroitness in using the hands,
body and mind

Dispose-to put in a particular place or order;
arranged; to get rid of; to sell

Incline- to deviate from the vertical or horizontal; to
have a mental tendency or preference

Incline-to attend in character or a course of action; to
lean; bend; to persuade; dispose; a sloping surface

92

Attendancy-a natural disposition; to move or act in some direction or toward some point or result

Place-position or situation; a proper or appropriate location position or time

Place-a building or location set aside for a specific purpose; a step or point in order of proceeding

Respond-to answer, reply

Sell-to promote or effect the sale; acceptance or approval of

Deviate-to turn aside or differ as from a course

Persuade-to prevail on a person to do something

9 781427 649324